BASKETBALL

► SCIENCE ◄

Written by
Logan Everett

CELEBRATION PRESS
Pearson Learning Group

Basketball is a **sport**. Basketball can also be a **science**.

If you look at basketball from a scientific point of view, you can improve your basketball game. Science can help you understand how a basketball bounces. It can also help you take better care of your body.

Scientists ask questions about everyday events. They observe how things happen and make guesses about why they happen that way. Then they test their guesses.

Scientists use their observations to ask questions and explore the answers. Here are some questions and answers about basketball.

Can science help you make more baskets?

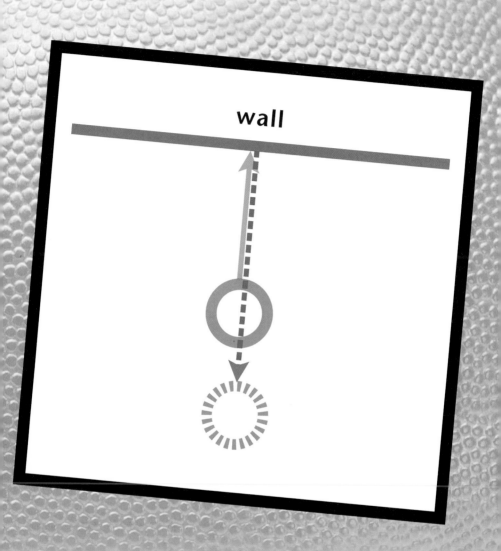

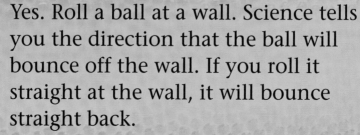 Yes. Roll a ball at a wall. Science tells you the direction that the ball will bounce off the wall. If you roll it straight at the wall, it will bounce straight back.

What if you roll the ball into the wall at an **angle**? Will the ball still bounce straight back?

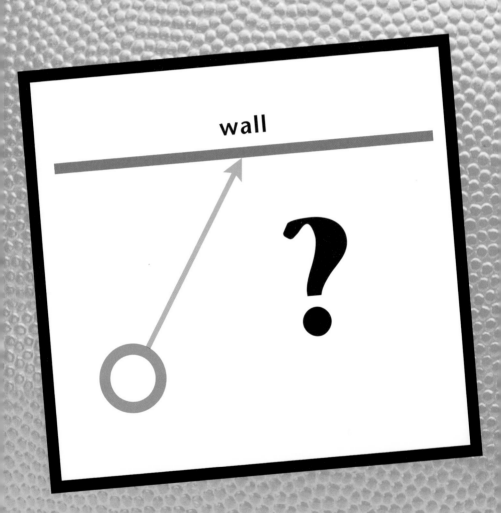

No, it won't. Science tells us that it will roll away from the wall at that same angle, but in the opposite direction.

9

Look at this **diagram**. Think about the people on the right who might get the ball after it hits the wall. Can you tell who will get the ball?

Think of the backboard as a wall. If the ball hits the wall just right, it will bounce off the wall just right. It will be a basket!

11

Can science help people **dribble** the ball?

Yes. Good dribbling takes lots of practice. Science tells us that the harder we push the ball, the harder it will bounce off the floor and the higher it will go. That's because a ball bounces back with about the same force you put into pushing it.

 Why do my **muscles** hurt after
I practice for a long time?

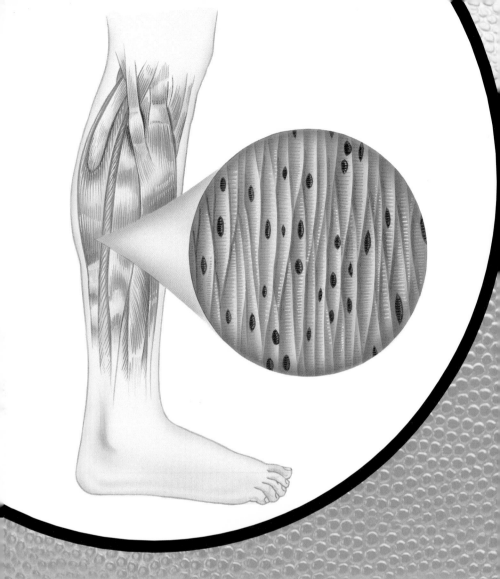

 Muscles help us move. They are made up of **fibers**. Fibers are a little like strings. Sometimes the muscles stretch too far. Some of the fibers can strain or tear. Then the muscles hurt until they heal.

Is there any way to protect muscles?

Yes. Stretch your muscles slowly and carefully before using them. Good basketball players stretch muscles slowly until they get a tight feeling. Then they hold each stretch. They don't bounce as they stretch. That could strain or tear the muscles.

 Why do people get so thirsty when they play basketball?

About two thirds of the human body is water! Your body loses lots of water when it sweats. Drinking liquids replaces the lost water. It's good to drink two or three quarts of water every day, even when you are not exercising.

 Why do basketball players sweat?

Your body sweats to cool itself down. The human body works best when its temperature is about 98 or 99 degrees Fahrenheit. Exercise can make the body heat up. If it gets too hot, you may get sick. So when the body heats up, it sweats. As the sweat dries, it cools the body.

Do you want to be a better basketball player?
Keep asking questions about the game. Then
try to find the answers. Books can help. So can
teachers and coaches. Exercise your muscles
and your brain and enjoy basketball science.

Glossary

angle the shape made when two lines meet at a point

diagram a simple picture that shows an idea

dribble to move a ball forward with a series of bounces

fibers stringlike cells that make up our muscles

muscles the body part that helps other body parts move

science knowledge based on facts that have been tested

sport an athletic game